POLK_ DOT POEMS

100 WEIRD AND WONDERFUL NATURE HAIKU

ZARO WEIL

ILLUSTRATED BY LUCY WYNNE

ZaZaKids
Books

CONTENTS

Tree

if I were as tall as you
as leafy
as old

I'd give away
all my shade
all summer

Cave

tunnel of big dark
do you really guard
all the dreams
of
all the world

Seagull

cruising cloud-curls
shrilling loud squarks
earthshaking sky things

to tell the sea

Platypus

flat yellow bill
brown furred back
smooth paddles
down river

blue velvet swirls

Hummingbird moth

what a fine long nose
what fun to smell
every shade of
every flower

Mushroom

popped up
this morning
in a blink

whoa

two blinks
another two dozen

Blossom

guessed your secret
I think you might just
burst into anything

like me

13

Patagonian mara

good golly
galloping rabbit
giggling giddy grins

great grass gobbler

Porcupine

if all your quills
were filled with ink
you could write
such sharp

porcupine tales

Spider

smart
spinning your own paths
criss-crossing the cosmos
thin thread
by
thin thread

Toad

moonshine crawl
slower-than-molasses
tongue flashing
lightning-time flicks

17

Wind

I know you are wild
  but are you free?
  yes!
      I think you are

just like
meeeeee

Superb lyrebird

if I could copy
any sound
like you
I'd sound
like the sun

laughing

Pangolin

scaly anteater
please
uncurl from that ball
don't be scared

bugs are small

Venezuelan poodle moth

button cute
fluffy white
big eyes
could I take you on

a little walk

Bubble

tiny ball of air

    inside

        water-whisper wall

gentleness afloat

Babirusa

fat fold after fold
mud roll after roll

'sublime fine time'

snorts this swine

29

Cloud

hundreds
thousands
millions
when whoosh
rolling off
in one
blockbuster
blow

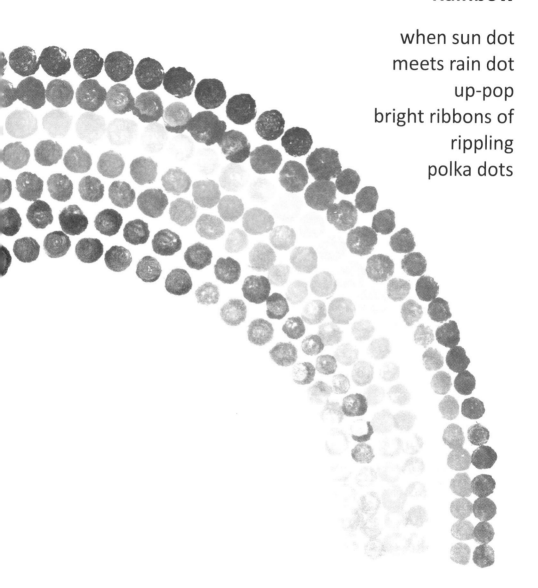

Rainbow

when sun dot
meets rain dot
up-pop
bright ribbons of
rippling
polka dots

Wombat

fuzzy wuzzy
digs a furrow
fuzzy wuzzy
loves a good
burrow

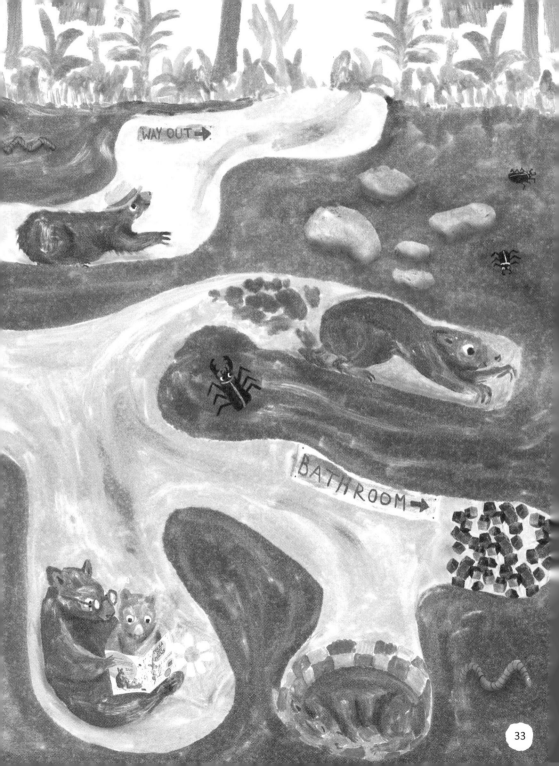

Parrotfish

what sharp teeth
how nice that you can
chomp yourself
a cosy place to live

Clam

slung in by the tide
sand-snug closed
shell
sun-cracks open

super beach day

Weed

amazing
explorer
popping up
in places
other plants

wouldn't dare

Hedgehog

asleep now
ball of spine ruffles
sunset falls
then all
snorts and snuffles

Zunzuncito

zigzagging
zany zooms
now sip your small sips
bird of a zillion
hums

Grass

barefoot soft
glitter green
a gift each spring

dandelions
included

Kitten

which is better
one kitten purring
two romping
or
three fluffy puffs

rolling roundabouts

Dumbo octopus

smooth slow sails
silent silk swirls
big ears soft-flapping

floating brollies

Gobi jerboa

such big ears
hearing everything
in the desert

even sand talking

Frog

slow-grow stars
   still water
      moon-slice

all ready for your noisy
   sing-song?

Rose

which came first
all colours of roses
or all the colours of

colours

Stone

poor stone
so all alone
but then
hundreds more
then
hundreds more

again

Dugong

sea cow tide-travels
through warm water
flippers drawing smooth

sea-doodles

Puffin

auk auk auk
how I talk talk talk
see my bright orange beak

now gawk gawk gawk

Sand

tiny grain between toes
teeny bit of rock
from long before

I was born

Star

when I see you
it's so true
if you can see me
bet
I twinkle too

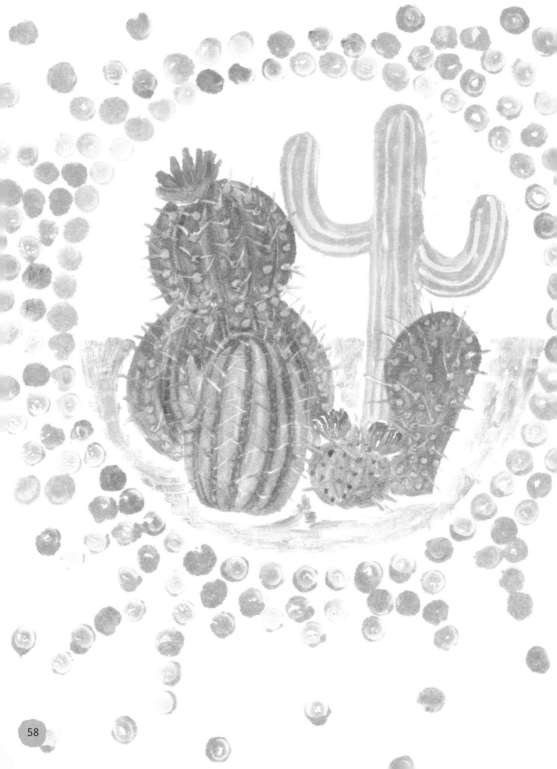

Cactus

prickly pronged
spongy smooth
flowering fat
water wizard

sun child

Apple

how many ways
can you say

good

how many ways
can you

thank earth

61

Hippopotamus

river-splashed
mud-drenched
fly-shooing beast
shimmies
water-drop halos

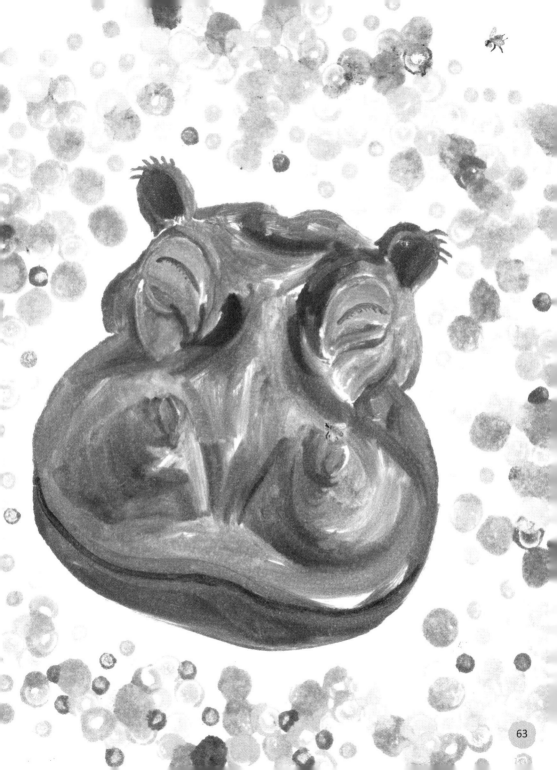

Rain

when all at once
streaming drops
each hurtling
towards a
heavenly

splash

Yeti crab

thoroughly white

white hair
white fingers
white claws
catching always
black sea

Fossa

long tail
sharp claws
leaping
from tree to tree to tree

you cat monkey you

Axolotl

magical beastie
becoming a brand new you

whenever you want

Sun

when you shine big
birds sing
flowers bloom
even mountains
spring up higher

Bluebird

is that you
on the high wire
no?
guess it's your
bippidy blue best friend

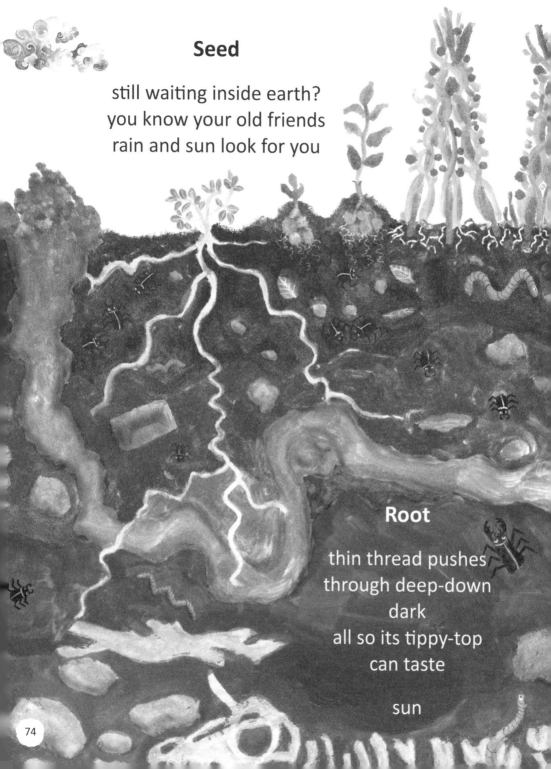

Seed

still waiting inside earth?
you know your old friends
rain and sun look for you

Root

thin thread pushes
through deep-down
dark
all so its tippy-top
can taste

sun

Waterfall

forever
tumbling down
but if you reversed
you'd be a
waterfly

Star-nosed mole

if I had your
pink starry nose

I'd smell the world
whiffle by sniffle

Beaver

slap chomp chew!
dam building you do!
stop!
game time!
splash!
water peekaboo!

Pine cone

rest here
little bird
or here
or here

see?

lots of us
on this
tree

Branch

wrapped in perfumed
sunbeam spray
branch
slow grows
unfurls leaf

unwraps blossom

Gerenuk

long long stretches
tall tall necks
fat fat nibbles
so so full

sleep sleep sleep

Goblin shark

ancient living fish
your sword-mouth
parts water
swims through
millions of years

Iguana

if there were
a scaly dinosaur
in my garden
it would look like you

bigger of course

Blue parrotfish

if I were
bright blue like you
I'd leap from the deep
and fly by

sky high

Clover

good morning
unfolds in four petals
were you always so

lucky green

Dog

floppy ears
bouncy pink tongue
what is it you want
            and
how huge a hug

Zebra duiker

black-striped
best mates
meander under
green canopy of
gold-striped

sun

Superb bird of paradise

spread that black
feather-cape
dazzle-bird
time to hop your
razzle-dance

Aye aye

please don't cry cry
you'll be hunting
bugs again
once the sun goes
bye bye

Moon

palest puff
in
just-night sky
that you?

of course
I spy your
crescent wisp

Bumblebee

wind-shaking buzz
all ready to grow
earth gardens

pollen whisperer

Daisy

in a surprise
cold up-jump
daisy appears
white petals

yellow smile

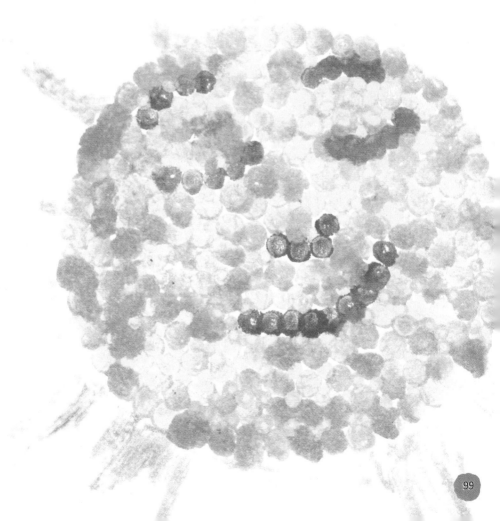

Light

oh!
I remember you
morning sun-breath
all a-whirl
through my window

Dust

if we were little
we'd be specks
like you
free-floating
uh oh!
achoo!

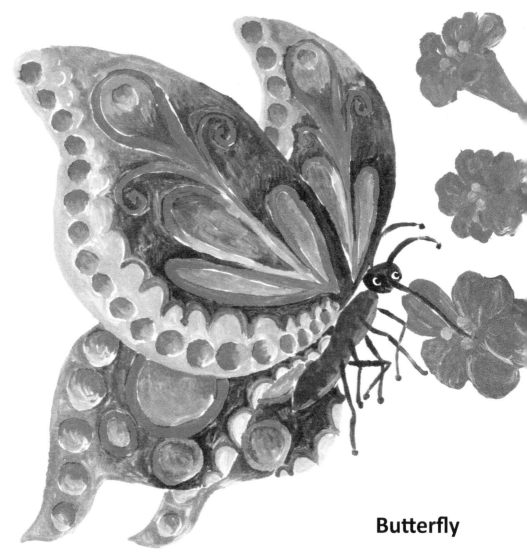

Stick insect

stillest bug
ever
how long have you been there
right in front of my nose

Butterfly

antennae quiver
sweet smells
soft wind-ride into
flower
nectar
bliss

Maned wolf

a stroll under stars
tapping earth
what?
a bug flies up
ready?

moon-leap

Sun bear

how perfect
your long long tongue
how sticky gold
that honey
you lap up

California condor

big bird
how can you fly so long
with no flaps

got it

you're an
airplane

Rattlesnake

sharp eyes
keen smell
earth-shaking rattle
glad I'm not a
mouse in a hole

Sea turtle

happy birthday
jurassic creature
how old?

millions of candle-lights

Seahorse

empty shell now
but once upon a time
you galloped off
through great waves

Lion

hail
king of beasts
do you truly tell
all the teensy ants
where to go

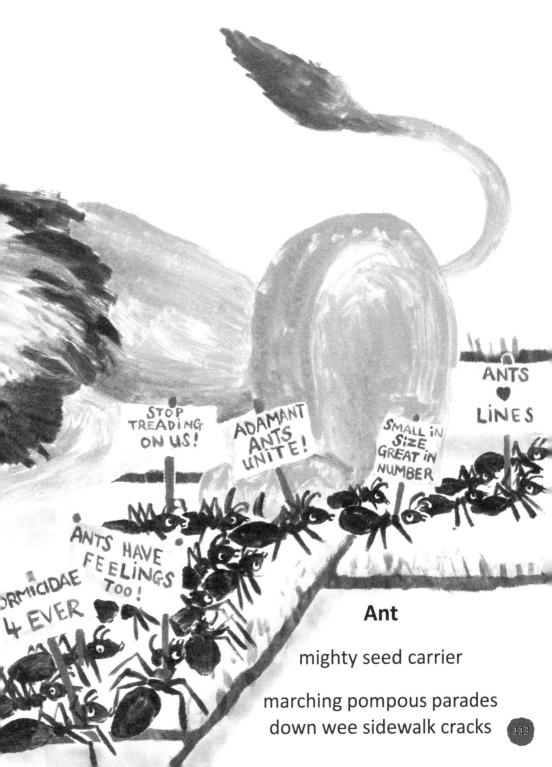

STOP TREADING ON US!

ADAMANT ANTS UNITE!

SMALL iN SiZE GREAT iN NUMBER

ANTS ♥ LINES

ANTS HAVE FEELiNGS TOO!

...ORMICIDAE 4 EVER

Ant

mighty seed carrier

marching pompous parades
down wee sidewalk cracks

113

Whale

once you walked on earth
then you swam in sea

blowhole breathing
mystery

Tide

do you know where
you are going
or
how long you'll be

I know

ask the moon

Snowflake

crystalline sky-ice
whirls twirls swirls
towards earth
spinning ever-white
candy-floss

Shadow

now I'm here
now gone
depends
how far
how long
light feels like
stretching me

Cherry blossom

watching
petal pink
sun-sprinkles
dreaming
big bowls
and
juicy red bites

118

Wild pig

wrapped in undergrowth
moonbeam
unwraps your power

hair bristles

fly hooves!

Kakapo

hush
night falls
dinner waits below
flightless wings
become
parachute things

Fog-basking beetle

what?
a headstand in desert sand?
catching water drops?

upside down?

Mountain

totally towering
did you just spring up
or was it a
long stretch

Dandelion

sky

these twilight petals
are for you
also
these puffy
blow-aways

Fog

even though
you soft-cover everything

I know you mostly
disappear into nothing

Sea pen

bright green quills
light up ocean floor
writing letters to fish
floating by

P.S. I Promise I won't eat you

Love from S.P.

Cricket

birds sing
lions roar
dogs bark
crickets ummm...
crickets ummm...
crickets cricket!

Daffodil

trembles
in
spring-blush wind
quivers all shades of
march-yellow
sunshine

131

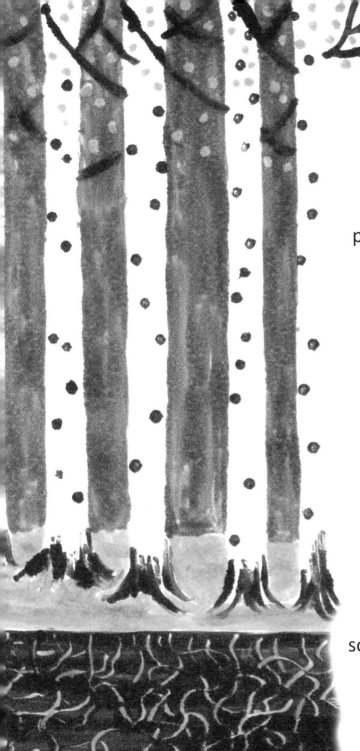

Forest

stretching
higher than high
pulsing roots through
juicy earth

deeper than deep

Moss

no flowers
no roots
just a green carpet

soft-hushing the forest

Mudpuppy

short legs
walking on slippery rock
crayfish swims by

water race!

TICKETS

Large: 1.00
Small: .50

START

Praying mantis

red green yellow
quick-changing
high-jumping
colours

painting the forest

Storm

forests snap
sea bubbles
mountains wobble
earth rip-roars to
madcap sky-song

Sloth

head turns slowly
all the way round
takes a long time
watching
everything

Pebble

so many pebbles
so many years
quietly crunching
underfoot

Thistle

seeds for birds
leaves for bugs
fluff for nests
nectar-spiked
flowered

giving plant

Heather

crayoned mauve clumps
decorate rolling hills
mobs of winter

sun-sequins

Horse

soft now
I hear your secret

'gallop wild
follow that unbridled wind'

AMAZING FACTS ABOUT SOME OF THE WEIRD AND WONDERFUL CREATURES

Platypus

This great-looking Australian egg-laying mammal hunts for food under water with its eyes and ears and nose completely closed. How does it find its prey? Aha! Its big, powerful yellow bill has thousands of little electrical receptor cells which enable it to find food and to hunt out the electric signals of all the aquatic creatures which might taste good. It's called electrolocation and it allows the platypus to snaffle up its food brilliantly. But it's hard to spot a platypus or talk to one because they are quite shy.

Hummingbird moth

Is it a bird? Is it an insect? Merrily buzzing from flower to flower, this tiny, speedy, wing-flapping, long-nosed, nectar-loving beastie has evolved to look a lot like a cute little hummingbird. But a hummingbird is a bird and this is a moth. Definitely not a bird. It is very smart because, by looking and acting like a bird, the hummingbird moth is able to stay safe from its predators who would have loved to eat it up for breakfast. This process, where one species grows up over thousands and thousands of years to look just like another species, is one of nature's brilliant tricks.

Patagonian mara

With strong limbs and long ears which are always standing at attention, this rodent who lives in the blowy grasslands of Argentina looks and acts like a racing hare. Maras are wildly fast and can run, hop and leap in great bursts of mind-boggling and dazzling speed as they search for tall yummy grasses to munch. And foxes and other predators to flee from. My advice is if you ever saw a mara and wanted to have a race, you shouldn't bother. They are too fast for any of us humans to catch up with in a million and one years.

Superb lyrebird

Not only are superb lyrebirds brilliant singers, their family is awesomely old – prehistoric really – and dates back to around 15 million years ago. Now these gorgeous, big ground-walking birds live in the colourful rainforests of Tasmania in Australia. The superb lyrebird just loves to sing all day. And what is particularly interesting is that it can copy the sounds of all the birds around it. But there's more. It can even imitate other sounds it hears in the forest. So, if you do go into the forest in Tasmania in Australia with a friend, and whisper a secret, the lyrebird would sing your secret out to everyone. So be careful where you go to tell your secrets.

Pangolin

Pangolins live in China and Africa. They are known as scaly anteaters because they are covered in sharp little scales which feel just like fingernails. When they are frightened they curl up into a scaly ball which you could almost hold in your hand (not a good idea). They are nocturnal and spend most of the day sleeping (curled up in balls), and then go smelling and foraging for food at night. They are hunted a lot so sadly there aren't a huge number of pangolins left in the world.

Venezualian poodle moth

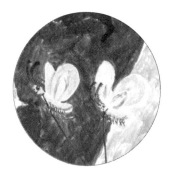

This little moth is one crazy creature. And until 2009 it was totally unknown in the world of zoology. . . the science where all kinds of creatures are observed and studied. Then one day a zoologist who was walking in a big national park in Brazil took a photo of this never-before-seen fluffy, googly-eyed, poodle looking moth and the world went gaga! A lot of other zoologists asked if it was really real, because they had never seen anything like it. Other scientists thought it was real. To tell you the truth, I don't have a clue. But I do know that it is adorable-looking in the photos. And that it would be a lot of fun to take this poodle moth on a little walk.

Babirusa

These hairy pig-like animals only live on four islands in Indonesia. They have long long tusks that curve beautifully upwards and the male babirusa's tusks keep growing during his whole life. They love to laze around in the rainforests by the banks of rivers. People in Indonesia love them. Too much. Because for years they have insisted on presenting their kings and queens with babirusas as gifts, so now there aren't a lot of them left. Which is sad. However, the government today are protecting them. So maybe, if you travel far away to Indonesia one day, you may come across one of these swine playing mud games by the river. But I would strongly advise you not to join in.

Wombat

If you went to Australia and visited Tasmania in the south east and looked at the ground really hard, you would find thousands of little holes and passageways dug by wombats. You see, wombats just love to be cosy. However, watch where you step, because wombats also make a lot of poop – about 80 or 100 cube-shaped pieces every night – which they like to stack up in poop hills outside their burrows so that other animals get the picture: KEEP OUT! PRIVATE! WOMBATLAND!!!!!

Parrotfish

If you were a coral reef at the bottom of a warm sea, you would LOVE parrotfish and want them to live around you and in you all the time. That is because parrotfish (there are 95 different varieties) just love to chomp away at algae and other poisons that smother and are harmful to coral reefs. In fact it is a superfish who swims around getting rid of coral's enemies. It goes wihout saying that parrotfish have incredible teeth. Fact is, it has some of the strongest and hardest on the planet. And what is phenomenal is that it has over 1000 teeth in its mouth arranged in 15 rows. Personally, I think it's better to be a human with only 32 teeth. Which is all you really need to eat a piece of chocolate cake.

Zunzuncito

The first thing to say about the brightly-coloured zunzuncito or bee hummingbird is that it is the smallest living bird in the whole wide world; just around the size of my pinkie. The second thing is that it only lives in Cuba. The third thing is that because it is so beautifully small, with a wonderful long bill, it can reach right inside a flower, sip the nectar and pick up some pollen dust. Then it takes that pollen and goes to visit another flower. It next deposits the pollen it is carrying to the new flower and starts the whole process again. Eventually, during a day, this plump little busybody bird can visit over 1500 flowers. So everybody gets some pollen. Which is what helps plants reproduce and grow.

Dumbo octopus

Deep deep deep down in the depth and freezing darkness of oceans all over the planet swims the rare dumbo octopus. (Once upon a time some scientist named these creatures after Disney's famous cartoon elephant named Dumbo. I guess it was because both had huge slow-flopping ears) The dumbo octopus uses its eight arms which are connected with webbing to glide through the inky water like a beautiful, smooth-flapping umbrella. And when a dumbo octopus gets hungry (which is most of the time) it uses its sensitive arms to detect little worms and crustaceans that live on or just above the ocean's floor. Next it pounces on them and swallows them whole. Because it lives so very deep in the water, human fishermen cannot catch it. So these lucky big beasties can stay safe and swim around flappy and happy every day.

Gobi jerboa

This curious little nocturnal rodent has the head of a mouse, whiskers like a cat, eyes like an owl, big ears like a hare, and kangaroo-strong long back legs. And if you saw one up close you might say, 'Oh. What big ears you have.' And it might reply. 'All the better to hear you with.' And it does have excellent hearing. The Gobi jerboa lives in the desert. It loves to sleep in its cosy burrow all day and then go out at night when it's cooler to forage for its dinner. This little furry weird-looking creature is also impressively strong and can leap more than two metres in the air and six metres on the ground. And could qualify, I am certain, for the 'Desert Animal Olympics'.

Dugong

The dugong is a gentle grey-brown giant swimming a slow path through warm coastal waters all around the world. A dugong spends most of its time grazing on underwater grasses at the bottom of the sea, and then every six minutes or so it rises up out of the water to take a little breath of air. Because, as a mammal, it needs to breathe air. Interestingly, this seafaring big, beautiful, mammal is related to another big, beautiful, mammal that lives on earth: the elephant. A long time ago sailors used to tell stories about strange sirens or mermaids in the sea who rose up to sing alluring songs. Today, people think these old seafarers may have actually seen dugongs when they were coming up for air. And who knows. Maybe long ago dugongs sang as well.

Puffin

Puffins are cute black and white little birds which live in the northern seas in colonies. They are powerful swimmers and can plunge into the cold sea deep down to find food. It's easy to hear puffins. They make a loud noise which sounds like auk-auk-auk. This author really loves puffins. She saw some in Iceland and couldn't help buying a few adorable stuffed puffin toys.

Yeti crab

This all white, blind, furry little crab was discovered in the South Pacific in 2005. It lives in the deepest parts of the ocean where there is no light. Now way way way down there all the yeti crabs in the neighbourhood cluster together, wiggling and writhing away as each crab tries to get close to the little warm water vents on the bottom of the sea. Oddly, the yeti's furry claw hairs grow the bacteria that yetis love to eat. Yep. The yeti grows its own food conviently right on its own arms. Imagine growing your own garden. . . on you!

Fossa

A word of warning! Beware the smooth-furred, light-brown fossa if you happen to be travelling to the island of Madagascar. This tree-climbing predator loves to eat other animals and is very good at it. With semi-retractable claws (good for climbing trees and jumping from tree to tree), flexible ankles (good for grasping tree trunks), a fabulously strong tail that it can swing around like a tightrope as it leaps through the trees, plus fearsome cat-like teeth, this large carnivore means business. But I think mostly it's lemurs and wild pigs and mice and a few others living in Madagascar who really need to be a-feared.

Axolotl

This creature is sometimes called a Mexican walking fish. But it is NOT a fish. It is a reptile. And the most amazing and I mean really amazing thing about the axolotl is that it can regrow itself to heal. So, for example, if it lost a leg on February 1, by Valentine's Day (February 14), that limb will have grown back. Absolutely perfectly. And more. It can also grow back its lungs, heart and even parts of its brain. Scientists and this author agree that the axolotl is one smart creature and deserves lots of study. So that maybe we humans can learn one day how to grow things back as well.

Star-nosed mole

This brown 5 inch long mole, who is mostly blind, has one of the most sensitive noses of any mammal in the world. . . 100,000 nerve fibres packed onto a little pink star-shaped nose which goes bopping different places on the ground up to twelve times every second! And when it finds a nice boneless invertebrate (like an insect or a worm) to eat, it can munch it up in less than one quarter of a second. It can also swim and can even smell things while in the water. This mole is really truly one astonishing little starry-nosed beastie.

Gerenuk

Imagine you are exploring around the Horn of Africa and you decide to take a little rest during the hot afternoon under some nearby trees. Well, you might be surprised to find yourself in the middle of a herd of beautiful, gentle, long-necked, small-headed, big-eyed, brown and black antelopes. Some of these antelopes might even have curly big horns. They would be the males. All of them would be busy grazing for yummy leaves, shoots, herbs and flowers. Some might even be standing up on their strong hind legs to get the goodies at the top of the trees. They are quite shy, but if you ask nicely, they might even stretch up and pluck a nice piece of fruit for you.

Goblin shark

What a bizarre-looking creature. With a snaggle-tooth jaw covering big nail-like teeth which can pop out to devour any passing food creature, this shark comes from a family who were swimming around way back 125 million years ago.

One of the wondrous things about this fish is that its skin is transparent. You can see right through it. Which means you can see all of its blood racing around. Which also means the goblin shark is the same colour as . . . wait for it . . . pink bubble-gum!

Iguana

These large lizards, who are often the wildest, brightest green imaginable, can live for 20 years or more. They love to sunbathe for a few minutes – but they are very hard to spot because they also love to streak like lightning over the ground, up walls, through trees, around stones and inside garbage bins (if there are people living closeby). Some people keep iguanas as pets. But they can't really house them in a normal shoebox since iguanas can grow up to 6 feet long (almost two meters).

Blue parrotfish

If you were to go to a great aquarium that somehow had a miniature coral reef at the bottom and pressed your nose to the glass to look at all the wonderful fish swimming around, I bet this one would catch your attention: the blue parrotfish. That might be because it is as true-blue as bluebells, blueberries or bluebirds. Like other parrotfishes, the blue variety loves to eat the algae which grows all over coral reefs. And once they have chomped it up with their 1000 hard teeth, they digest it and – like magic – it comes out the other end as pure white sand. Who knew!

Zebra duiker

I think the next time I look for a cute stuffed animal to give some kids I know, I would ask the shop if they had any zebra duikers. The real life zebra duiker is a little black-striped, golden-brown antelope who lives in rainforests along the western coast of Africa. It is quite shy and tends to graze in pairs on fruit, seeds and whatever nice leaves it can find. Its black stripes help it to blend in with the shadows under the trees and protect it from predators.

Superb bird of paradise

Say you decide to visit New Guinea and go adventuring in the rainforests there. My guess is that before an hour goes by you'll have heard a curious-sounding bird call. Investigating, you'll spot a gorgeous jet-black little male bird scrubbing the dirt with a branch of leaves. Of course you'll hide behind a tree and watch in astonishment. A few curious females approach. After this bird has prepared his dance floor, he will dramatically open out his neck feathers into a gorgeous black cape which he will lift up over his head to reveal a splendid bright-green shiny chest. Next he'll hop and dance in wacky, non-stop circles. But in the end it is no use. The females will say they are not interested and hip-hop away. Poor bird. But he will dance again. And again and again till he finds his mate.

Aye aye

Strange strange and triple strange! This rare and weird-looking little creature lives only in jungly Madagascar and likes to do pretty much everything (like eating and sleeping and hanging out) way up in the trees. It is nocturnal and only goes looking for dinner at night. It has an extraordinary supersonic feature called echolocation (the same system bats use, a bit like animal radar) to find its prey. As soon as it spots something, it taps-taps-taps somewhere on the bark of a tree. Then it uses its long two front teeth to gnaw a teeny tiny hole in the bark. Finally it puts its thin, long middle finger right inside the little hole and pulls out a few delicious grubs to eat. What's even more bizarre is that some people in Madagascar are frightened of aye ayes, probably because they look so oddball. But they don't really need to be because aye ayes just go around doing what aye ayes do. However, little grubs living inside trees in Madagascar should definitely be frightened.

Stick insect

A long time ago, this clever insect learned to stay safe by evolving to look just like a twig on a tree, the same grey-brown colour to blend in and even the same little lichen-looking speckles. However, if the stick insect is threatened by a bird or a mouse who wants dinner, not only does it stay perfectly still, it can drop off from its perch right to the ground. And lie there playing dead. Then the hungry creatures, looking for something alive, will leave it alone. And we humans think we are smart!

Maned wolf

News flash! The maned wolf is a dog. The largest dog variety in South America. And at twilight time, it comes out of its burrow and using its long ears listens for small animals or insects in the grass. Next it taps the ground with one of its long legs until the hidden creature or insect comes out. And wham. With a couple of big bites, the maned wolf gobbles up its prey. It also eats seeds and nuts which it later eliminates in its poop. Now this is a good thing in nature because it means that the seeds can be spread and happily grow in new places. And that is how our ecosystem flourishes.

Sun bear

I love sun bears. These brown or black bears who live in rainforests, are the smallest, cutest and cuddliest bears in the world. They are called sun bears because they have a patch of light yellow fur on their chests which looks just like the sun rising. They also have the longest tongue imaginable, a full 12 inches or 30 cm! And with curved strong claws and great big paws, they are fantastic climbers. Another exciting thing about these bears is that they can smell things 2000 times better than you and me. Incredible! In conclusion, sun bears are absolutely adorable and this author really wishes she could meet one.

California condor

This magnificent creature is the largest flying bird in North America. It has a wingspan of 10 feet or 309 cm. And if you were in California and looked up you might be lucky enough to spot one cruising through the sky way up at 4,600 metres and flying 90 kilometres an hour! In fact, the California condor doesn't really flap its wings very much so you might even think you were looking at a small airplane. This giant bird is extremely rare and was almost extinct. But now, there are several sanctuaries dedicated to the recovery of this extraordinary bird species.

Sea turtle

If you get into a boat and sail the sea – especially a sea in a tropical or sub-tropical part of the planet – and then look underneath the rolling waves, you might spy a sea turtle swimming smoothly through the water like a beautiful dream. Some people call them marine turtles. These huge and magnificent reptiles with flippers (there are seven different species) can trace their family tree back over 100 million years. Hard to imagine! That makes them one of the oldest animal families on the planet.

Seahorse

Seahorses are tiny and beautiful fish with a little head that looks like a horse and a long tail made of cute squares that rotate. It doesn't swim flat but floats and bobs around in the water standing up. It is very scaly and bony so most other sea creatures don't bother to chase it for food because it doesn't taste very good. Which is a good thing since seahorses swim very very slowly. Another strange thing is that its two eyes rotate independently which means it can look forward and backwards at the same time! It can can also change colour whenever it feels like it. And one more unusual thing is that it is the father who has the baby seahorses, which are called fry. A bit like small fry!

Wild pig

If you have a look at a map of the world, close your eyes and point to loads of places on the globe, you'll probably find a lot of wild boars running around at night. This big beast is also called a wild pig or wild swine and is related to cute little pink pigs. But this version is bulky, with blackish-brown grizzly hair, long razor-sharp tusks and short legs that can whoosh through the countryside like the wind. It is also very smart and goes around in marauding groups in the darkness searching for roots, bulbs, nuts, berries, eggs, frogs and more. Clear fact. . .I certainly would not want to meet a boar in the woods at night. Not for all the juicy worms in the world.

Kakapo

This fluffy yellow-green bird, who lives in New Zealand, is called an owl parrot and is a curious creature. 1. It does not fly. 2. It is the heaviest, fattest parrot in the world. 3. It lives for up to 100 years. 4. It is a great climber and when it wants to eat something that is lying under a tree at night, it uses its wings as a parachute and glides from the top of the tree right down to the earth. 5. It has strong legs and can waddle along the ground a long way to find food. The sad thing is, kakapos are almost extinct. There are maybe a hundred left in the world. But the good news is scientists are trying hard to protect them.

Fog-basking beetle

Picture this. Once a year, for thirty days in a row, a strange fog rolls over the desert. It is the only water that the desert ever gets. And it is just water vapour at that. Not easy to drink. But this brainy beetle has managed to figure out how to capture the tiny droplets and quench its thirst. It does this by climbing to the top of sand dunes and facing the wind with its back in the air, it then turns its body upside down and uses its little forewings as tiny water collectors. . . and shazam! Water droplets form and roll down into its mouth. A perfect desert operation.

Sea pen

This beautiful and complicated creature, which hardly ever moves, lives at the bottom of the deep sea. It looks like it is planted there because it has a base that anchors it into the ground and little suckers called polyps. Each polyp has eight tentacles which wave about in the dark water searching for plankton which it loves to eat. It comes in beautiful colours; yellow, orange, red and brown and if anything touches it, it glows like a light bulb switched on under water.

Mudpuppy

Believe it or not, this puppy is not really a dog. Maybe it's called mudpuppy because some people think it sounds like a puppy making its squeaky little bark. This rusty-coloured amphibian has its gills (which look like a fluffy feathery collar) around its neck. It mostly lives in the bottoms of lakes, ponds and streams. When the mudpuppy moves, it uses a combination of walking and propelling itself side-to-side in the water. A bit like a wind-up toy. But don't let it hear you say that.

Praying mantis

Aha! Beware the praying mantis. It may look harmless, like it is just sitting quietly and meditating; watching the world go by. Well, it would be more accurate to say it is just watching the world go by so it can pounce on something yummy and swallow it for dinner. With incredible bulgy eyes, a body as agile as a cat and with the ability to rotate its head without moving anything else, this cunning little beastie is one clever pint-sized predator. So seriously. BEWARE!! It bites!

Sloth

This author really saw a sloth. Up close. It was hanging from a tree near the swimming pool where we were lounging. In South America. It hardly moved. It was very furry and had very long legs and a cute smiley kind of rounded face. Sloths are very strong and can hang on to their place on a branch for a long time. Even sleep there. And if a jaguar should come by on the prowl and try to get the sloth off the tree, it would not be able to budge it at all. Now this is startling. When sloths poop, they only do it once a week. They travel slowly down the tree to the base and wiggle around to dig a little toilet hole. And just like that, the job is done. Easy peasy.

Published by ZaZaKids Books
in association with Troika Books

First published 2021

1 3 5 7 9 10 8 6 4 2

A CIP catalogue record for this book is available
from the British Library

ISBN: 978-1-909991-15-6

Printed in Poland

Designed by Sarah Pyke

Troika Books Ltd.
Well House, Green Lane,
Ardleigh CO7 7PD, UK
www.troikabooks.com

ZaZaKids Books
www.zazakidsbooks.com